The
Cotswold Way

Mark Richards

The Devil's Chimney

Published by
REARDON & SON

56, Upper Norwood Street, Leckhampton,
CHELTENHAM, Gloucestershire   GL53 ODU

Copyright © 1995

REARDON & SON

Fully Revised Second Edition 1996

Written and Illustrated
by MARK RICHARDS

Cover design from a watercolour of Uley church
by DAVID BELLAMY

ISBN 1 873877 10 2

Copyright © 1995
MARK RICHARDS

Printed by STOATE & BISHOP (Printers) Ltd.
CHELTENHAM, Glos.

Introduction

The Cotswolds are my home ground, born and bred into farming, I have tilled the soil and raised cattle upon its broad pastures for the main part of my life. The scenic meanderings of the Cotswold Way were first woven into my life in 1972 when I explored the newly established long distance path and wrote the very first guide. In 1983 I wrote a northbound guide for Penguin Books to compliment the southbound 'little green book', as it became known, published by Thornhill Press: the Penguin guide flourishes still, while the Thornhill guide was finally laid to rest last year after twenty-one years service with sales in excess of fifty thousand copies.

So this present guide, co-incidently sustaining the eleven year cycle of origination, sets course with re-newed vigour, bolstered by the prospect that the Cotswold Way is destined to become a National Trail. Thus more deeply embedded into the fabric of the Cotswold landscape. The crucial formal consultation, conducted by Virginia Richardson the Cotswold Way Development Officer, began Spring 1995.

The broad Cotswold region is already recognised for the distinctive quality of its landscape for in 1968 it was designated an 'Area of Outstanding Natural Beauty', further enlarged in 1991 to its currrent 790 sq. miles, making it the largest of the forty AONBs in England and Wales. It forms the broadest, highest and most strikingly coherent element of the Jurassic Limestone belt running on a diagonal course from the Humber estuary to the Dorset coast. This particular form of limestone is known as Oolite, due to the roe-egg form of the deposits held in the finely grained stone. A stone that has handsomely served architects and masons down the centuries featuring in many of the finest buildings in the land, from the university colleges in Oxford and major buildings of state in London, down to the natural order of church, manor, cottage and barn.

The 104 mile Cotswold Way winds up and down the west-facing escarpment, analogous to a coastal path - the Cotswold Edge akin to a clifftop, tantalising the walker's eye with a panoramic sweep of the Evesham and Severn Vales, and too the distant rolling hillscape into the Welsh Marches. Consistent and familar features in view are the Malvern Hills, the pudding-shaped May Hill with its clump of trees and beyond the sinuous silver streak of the tidal Severn and the dark undulating line of the Forest of Dean.

The origins of the Cotswold Way go back to 1950 when the concept was first mooted by the then Gloucestershire District Committee of the Ramblers' Association West of England area, under the enthusiastic secretaryship of Tony Drake. The National Parks and Access to the Countryside Act of 1949 had laid stress on the need for a full survey of rights-of-way by County Councils and made provision for the establishment of long distance routes such as the Pennine Way, Offa's Dyke and the Thames Towpath.

The Midlands area of the R.A. proposed a long distance route from The Wrekin to the Forest of Dean and Graham Lentel came forward with details of a route from Broadway to Stroud via the dip slope wolds.

A sub-committee met on February 20th 1951 and decided that a route along the escarpment to be called the "Cotswold Edge Way" was preferable to the Lentel route and was more likely to be popular. The concept was greeted with favour at the National Parks Commission, but they were not ready to further its cause until other more prestigious routes were realised.

The dawning came in 1968 when the Gloucestershire County Council Planning Department produced a countryside recreation study. Two years later with modest pomp they designated the Cotswold Way using existing rights-of-way and a trifle too much road walking. The entire route was signposted, and in close co-operation between the R.A. and Cotswold Warden Service was waymarked in a joint operation codenamed "Operation Cotswaymark". To every waymark was added a distinguishing white dot. The launch coincided with the Ramblers' Association Footpath Week.

As a postscript, remarkably Tony Drake remains the Gloucestershire R.A. Footpath Secretary, as dogged as ever in his defence of public access to the Gloucestershire countryside. Furthermore, 1995 marks both the Silver Jubilee of the Cotswold Way and Diamond Jubilee of the Ramblers' Association.

This guide reflects the dynamics of a trail in transition. Included are several exciting new alignments, all subtle changes that use existing rights-of-way, though not yet specifically waymarked, they are conventionally waymarked, and are definite improvements.

The Cotswold Way is one of the finest excuses for a day in the country that England has to offer. Cast off your concerns, banish your worries and walk free through this rural wonderland - go on !

Helen tries the Drake Seat on Cleeve Common, In the background are Nottingham Hill and the distinctive outline of the Malvern range.

4

For the broader perspective it is always wise for the walker to consult Ordnance Survey maps, they are, after all, in some form or another my constant companions. Alternatively, should you wish to wander further afield then PATHFINDER sheets 1043, 1067, 1066, 1089, 1113, 1112, 1132, 1151, 1167, 1183 are invaluable. For route planning there is no peer to the LANDRANGER series, the following sheets cover the route 150, 151, 162, 163, 172.

In researching this guide the author had the pleasure of using extracts from the first six-inch survey of 1881 (northern half): and 1890 edition (south of Dursley). It is fascinating to witness the changes and record them, however narrow the span of attention.

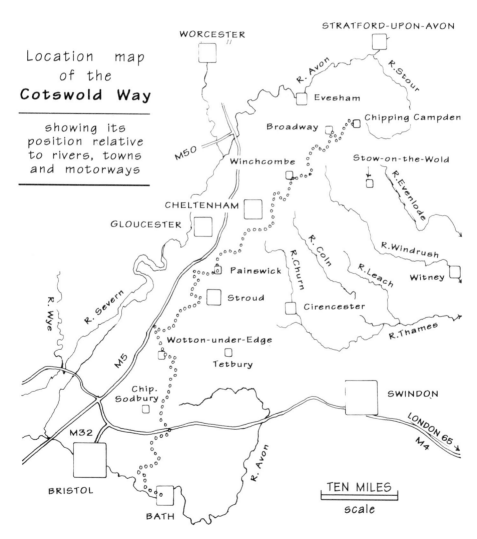

Location map of the **Cotswold Way**

showing its position relative to rivers, towns and motorways

The strip-map in this guide is based upon the original six-inch Ordnance Survey, with selected deletions and observed additions. So, whilst the map is deficient of many incidental and contemporary features, the effect has been to provide a simple walker-friendly aid to navigation. The maps show roads, field boundaries, woodland and selected buildings. The Way is defined by little circles, where the route accompanies a footpath two dots intervene, a bridleway a dash and where the route follows a road then only the circles show. Other paths and tracks are shown by respective dot and dash convention. The maps are numbered and every mile marked to give a 'yardstick' of progress.

Initials have been used on the strip-maps to indicate obstacles thus:

s = stile, g = hand or bridle-gate,
k = kissing-gate, G = field-gate, fb = footbridge.

Anyone contemplating walking the Cotswold Way is strongly recommended to acquire 'THE COTSWOLD WAY HANDBOOK' produced by the Gloucestershire Area of the Ramblers' Association. This annually up-dated reference gives sound logistical advice together with details of accommodation and travel. It is on sale in local bookshops and Tourist Offices or via Reardon Publishing (address at rear of this book).

For general visitor advice contact the Tourist Information Offices at :

(s) = seasonal opening

BROADWAY (s)	Cotswold Court, The Green	01386 - 852937
CIRENCESTER	Corn Hall, Market Place	01285 - 654180
CHELTENHAM	77 The Promenade	01242 - 522878
WINCHCOMBE	Town Hall, North Street	01242 - 602925
STOW-ON-THE-WOLD	Hollis House, The Square	01451 - 831082
GLOUCESTER	St Michael's Tower, The Cross	01452 - 421188
STROUD	George Street	01453 - 765768
TETBURY (s)	Old Courthouse, 47 Long Street	01666 - 503552
BATH	Abbey Chambers, Abbey Churchyard	01225 - 462831
BRISTOL	St Nicholas Church, St Nicholas Street	01117 - 9260767

The Cotswold Way is part of a marvellous network of footpaths and bridleways providing access opportunities to the Cotswolds and near country. Many of these rights-of-way also function as separate, often specifically waymarked, circular walks, encouraging active visitors to venture laterally to discover the richness of the English countryside. If you would like to learn about the ways of the countryside, but are a little uncertain with a map or prefer not to walk alone, then the Countryside Service provides a regular programme of guided walks led by knowledgeable members of the Cotswold Voluntary Warden Service. The walks are free though donations are welcomed, for the latest walks programme contact : The Cotswold Countryside Service, County Planning Department, Gloucestershire County Council, Shire Hall, Gloucester GL1 2TN - 01452-425674.

Manorway,   Stanton

CHIPPING CAMPDEN TO BATH

Concisely mapped and illustrated route description
with mileage 65 shown from Chipping Campden

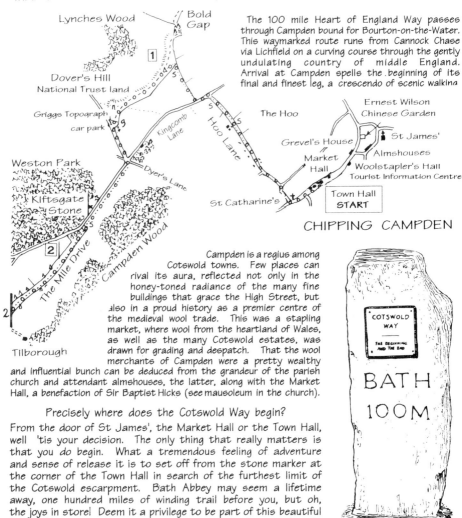

The 100 mile Heart of England Way passes through Campden bound for Bourton-on-the-Water. This waymarked route runs from Cannock Chase via Lichfield on a curving course through the gently undulating country of middle England. Arrival at Campden spells the beginning of its final and finest leg, a crescendo of scenic walking

CHIPPING CAMPDEN

Campden is a regius among Cotswold towns. Few places can rival its aura, reflected not only in the honey-toned radiance of the many fine buildings that grace the High Street, but also in a proud history as a premier centre of the medieval wool trade. This was a stapling market, where wool from the heartland of Wales, as well as the many Cotswold estates, was drawn for grading and despatch. That the wool merchants of Campden were a pretty wealthy and influential bunch can be deduced from the grandeur of the parish church and attendant almshouses, the latter, along with the Market Hall, a benefaction of Sir Baptist Hicks (see mausoleum in the church).

Precisely where does the Cotswold Way begin?

From the door of St James', the Market Hall or the Town Hall, well 'tis your decision. The only thing that really matters is that you *do* begin. What a tremendous feeling of adventure and sense of release it is to set off from the stone marker at the corner of the Town Hall in search of the furthest limit of the Cotswold escarpment. Bath Abbey may seem a lifetime away, one hundred miles of winding trail before you, but oh, the joys in store! Deem it a privilege to be part of this beautiful Cotswold countryside, a treat whether you walk alone or share it with good companions.   Bon voyage.

Walk west along the High Street, turning right at St Catharine's Catholic Church and as the road bends into Back Lane bear left up Hoo Lane, where this becomes a green lane. The bridle- and foot-paths are segregated for the mutal comfort. Reaching Kingcomb Lane go left then right along a field edge path with a hedge to the right to reach a stile between two ash trees. The great escarpment amphitheatre of Dover's Hill is now at hand. Pass the O.S. column and reaching the scarp survey the broad, fertile chequer-board of the Vale of Evesham. Walk left along the sheep cropped edge to the Griggs Topograph, a fine viewpoint. An American friend once likened the scene to that at Little Bighorn in Montana, where in 1876 General Custer made his ill-judged 'last stand' against over-whelming numbers of Sioux Indians. Leave this National Trust property, passing through the car park, going left upon the road, then right at the cross-roads, making sure you slip over the verge onto the headland of the arable field, rather than along the verge of the road. A stone stile puts you into a small enclosure. Bear left to a wall gap with a brief passage of woodland heralding entry into The Mile Drive, a broad gently winding meadow, originally an estate leisure carriage-drive.

The Market Hall

Griggs Topograph on Dover's Hill

William Grevel's House in Campden High Street

MAP 2   THE MILE DRIVE to BROADWAY

The Way keeps close to the lefthand hedge for precisely one mile, and as a track slips left towards farm buildings the footpath crosses a wall-stile at the junction of three parish boundaries. This wall's north/south alignment also perpetuates the course of Ryknild Street, a Roman road which ran from Wall in Staffordshire to link up with the Fosse Way at Bourton-on-the-Water. Despite its suffix, Buckle Street, sometimes termed Buggildway, is not Roman. It came into being as an Anglo-Saxon trading route linking the Vale with the high Cotswolds. The name Buckle derives from a Saxon lady landowner called Burghild.

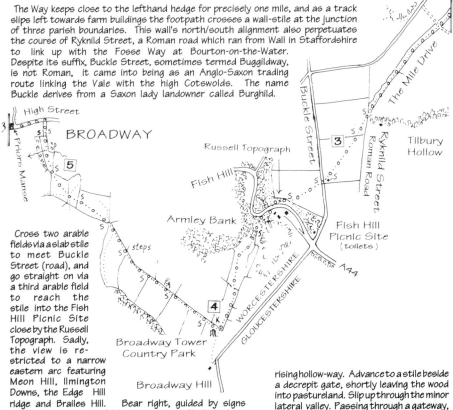

Cross two arable fields via a slab stile to meet Buckle Street (road), and go straight on via a third arable field to reach the stile into the Fish Hill Picnic Site close by the Russell Topograph. Sadly, the view is restricted to a narrow eastern arc featuring Meon Hill, Ilmington Downs, the Edge Hill ridge and Brailes Hill. Bear right, guided by signs cautiously cross the A44 at its brow. Climb a short bank onto a track, and almost at once bear off right along a thin path which swings left in light woodland to join a

rising hollow-way. Advance to a stile beside a decrepit gate, shortly leaving the wood into pastureland. Slip up through the minor lateral valley. Passing through a gateway, keep to the left-hand flank of the lateral valley dappled by hawthorn scrub to a stile directly below Broadway Tower.

Broadway Tower stands at an elevation of 1024ft/312m. The tall kissing-gate immediately at hand affords entry to the Broadway Tower Country Park, with facilities for picnics and quiet enjoyment of its splendid elevated setting, obtain an entry fee from Tower shop. During its descent from Broadway Tower the Way accompanies a wall. Pause at the seat prior to the steps to survey Burhill and the vale towards Bredon Hill.

Continue down the rough pasture to a hurdle and stile. Now with the field boundary to the left, pass via a mid-hedge stile to bear half right to a stile in the corner, with orchards on either hand. Advance to cross a stream rising within the small pasture, pass through a small yard via stiles into a lane, enter Broadway High Street, and go left.

Russell   Topograph

Broadway Tower has a peerless panorama and fully merits the modest entry fee to gaze from the battlements across the broad vale. It was built as a landmark folly in 1800 by the Earl of Coventry from his seat at Croome Court beyond Pershore, by which he could then pinpoint his hunting lodge estate of Springhill. Climb up and feast your eyes.

MAP 3   BROADWAY to LAVERTON HILL

Wend down this street, one of the most photographed village thoroughfares in England. Welcome the day that the traffic is calmed to a trickle, though a scourge on all talk of a by-pass, as it would only take away the charming back-door countryside from Broadway and bequeath little in return. The famous visitor appeal of the village has been cultivated and you'll do well to avoid being enticed into some shop or inn, a personal weakness being Jelfs' - a veritable treasure-house.

Walk down via the Green and go left along Church Road (the way to Snowshill and its much admired Manor House). Over the way is the well screened Abbots Grange, the oldest house in Broadway. The footway passes Church Close, entrance to the new car park facility, and St Michael's and All Angels Church, a Victorian replacement for the C12th St Eadburgha's. Cross over just before the gracious Austin House, passing down a short lane on the right. From the kissing-gate cross the cattle pasture, advance to a handsome stone footbridge spanning Broadway Brook, a tributary of Badsey Brook and thence the Avon. The footbridge was built by the ever active northern group of the Voluntary Warden Service.

The footpath continues through the ensuing sheep pasture to a stile onto West End Lane. Go straight across to the left-hand stile, entering a path that rises beside a hedge confined by fencing. At the top a stile leads into a sheep pasture. Continue the ascent beside the right-hand hedge curving under Broadway Coppice to the hand-gate at the top. The Way rises to join a track merging from the right. In due course bear right, crossing the head of an old hollow-way to reach a hand-gate, at a further path junction exit the woodland. Keep to the left-hand edge of this arable field advancing beside the hedge, with the first glimpse of the three masts on Cleeve Common appearing to the south-west.

Cross a stile beside a white gate, then glance past the projecting pair of gates to another stile, which puts the path on the left side of the fence. Continue beyond the shed to a stile in the field corner, enjoying the pleasing view down the combe towards Buckland. Here the Way re-enters Gloucestershire. Exit the short lane enclosure by a novel cross-corner stile into the fenced lane. Proceed left (south) reaching a gate at the lane's end and take the stile to its left. Don't allow the apparent options to confuse you - the fenced path offers stiles to left and right and a way forward, however, the Way goes immediately right, which simply puts you beyond the lane end gate. Bear right beside the fence via a very decrepit field gate, henceforward, accompany the fence via two more gates, with glimpses over Buckland and across the Evesham Vale. Enter a fenced trackway leading onto Laverton Hill.

Despite the recent imposition of fencing on this passage, wayfarers can feel for the first time bedrock underfoot and the sense of being on an ancient trackway. The broad views are a compensation for not visiting the attractive scarp-foot villages of Buckland and Laverton. Snowshill makes the briefest of appearances - as a reminder of a place you just must visit someday, for the handsome Manor and the Snowshill Arms!

Burhill is a sub-scarp spur, destined in geological time to become an outlying hill, after the manner of Dumbleton and Bredon. On the human scale of history, yet still distant past, the plateau was defended in Iron Age times, forming an important hill-fort refuge for people tilling the fertile vale, hence its 'burg' name.

Broadway has quite a selection of hostelries for the indulgence of visitors. Cotswold Way travellers may find the Crown and Trumpet, near St Michael's, just about ideal for a quiet repast ahead of the steady climb to Shenberrow Hill.

BROADWAY

Lygon Arms

Jelfs Newsagents

A44

Abbots Grange

St Michael's

West End Lane

Sfb

Church Close car park & toilets

Broadway Coppice

West End

SNOWSHILL

Burhill Iron Age hill-fort

Buckland Wood

Laverton Hill Barn

Jelfs' charming shopfront

The Lygon Arms

MAP 4   LAVERTON HILL to BECKBURY

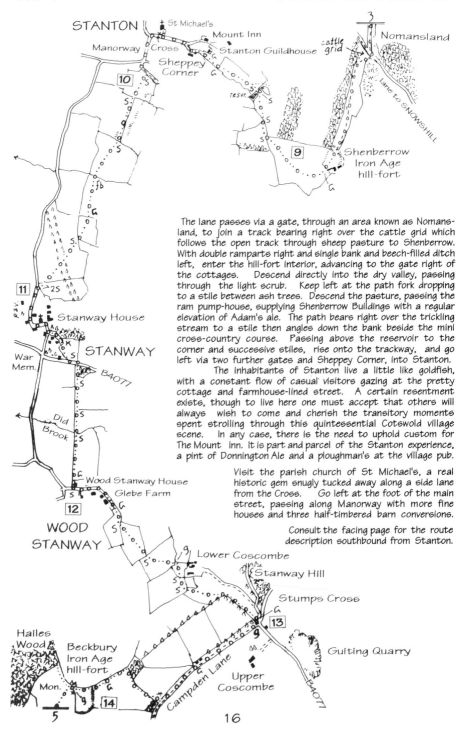

The lane passes via a gate, through an area known as Nomansland, to join a track bearing right over the cattle grid which follows the open track through sheep pasture to Shenberrow. With double ramparts right and single bank and beech-filled ditch left, enter the hill-fort interior, advancing to the gate right of the cottages. Descend directly into the dry valley, passing through the light scrub. Keep left at the path fork dropping to a stile between ash trees. Descend the pasture, passing the ram pump-house, supplying Shenberrow Buildings with a regular elevation of Adam's ale. The path bears right over the trickling stream to a stile then angles down the bank beside the mini cross-country course. Passing above the reservoir to the corner and successive stiles, rise onto the trackway, and go left via two further gates and Sheppey Corner, into Stanton.

The inhabitants of Stanton live a little like goldfish, with a constant flow of casual visitors gazing at the pretty cottage and farmhouse-lined street. A certain resentment exists, though to live here one must accept that others will always wish to come and cherish the transitory moments spent strolling through this quintessential Cotswold village scene. In any case, there is the need to uphold custom for The Mount Inn. It is part and parcel of the Stanton experience, a pint of Donnington Ale and a ploughman's at the village pub.

Visit the parish church of St Michael's, a real historic gem snugly tucked away along a side lane from the Cross. Go left at the foot of the main street, passing along Manorway with more fine houses and three half-timbered barn conversions.

Consult the facing page for the route description southbound from Stanton.

Shenberrow   hill-fort

At the end of Manorway the road bends right and the Way passes straight along the short private road signed Chestnut Farm. The stile at the end puts the walker into pasture. Walk south on a discernible path; notice the landslipped slump over to the left as you approach the stile. Now with the hedge to the left and arable land on the right, advance to a slipped bank in the next corner. The stile sets the path into a cattle pasture, an abundance of thistles flanks the path. A footbridge eases the path through the bramble-choked stream and on into sheep pasture to a gate in a fence, the path bearing slightly right to a stile into parkland cattle pasture. The path trends diagonally half-left across the oak and horse-chestnut avenue via two fence stiles to emerge onto the minor road. Go left through Stanway.

Notice on the right, the cricket pavilion set upon staddle stones to prevent rodents from 'holing-out' the equipment stored within. Admire the tithe barn, which now serves as the village hall, the parish church of St Peter's and of course Stanway House, as fine a mansion as Cotswold stone can fashion, the gate-house a sumptuously stylish addition.

The Way departs left at the great yew. Stroll past a cottage to quite the most handsome kissing-gate on the entire Cotswold Way. Wend on up the slope to the double gates onto the road footway, go left and shortly right, initially beside woodland. The path makes steady progression south via stiles with the hedge to the right. The last field has a fine sweeping ridge-and-furrow. A gate gives entry into a short lane by Wood Stanway House to reach a stile onto the road.

Walkers seeking a swifter progression may be attracted to the footpath that runs through the pastures below Hailes Wood directly to the Saltway at Hailes. The scenic merits of the ascent far outweigh the virtue of speed, so keeping faith with the waymarked route, go left, rising with the road access to Glebe Farm, the succeeding farm lane leads to a gate. The Way now sets about the steady ascent of a succession of pastures. Rise to a stile on the left, beside a crumpled gate, continue uphill to a stile, then pass along a ridge and furrow alignment to a hand-gate. Bear right up the bank to a fence stile rising above Lower Coscombe to a tall ladder-stile. Follow the wall-side track till ushered half-right up the scarp bank. At the crest, turn back and survey a grand prospect of wooded, sheep-grazed slopes. The edge-top path leads left to the double-gates onto the verge at Stumps Cross.

Go right via the hand-gate embarking on the farm track of Campden Lane, which leads to a group of old farm buildings at a gate. Notice the metal-sheeted shed set upon seven staddle stones and the dry mere sliced through by two walls which enabled farm stock to take water from four sides. Pursue the trackway beyond the buildings. This is a true Cotswold 'white way', probably as old as anything of man's landscape effects, a natural dry-ridgeway path traversed by shepherds, priests and tradesmen down every age. Looking north-east you can see David Nicholson's National Hunt training course running onto Cutsdean Hill beyond Guiting Quarry. On reaching a mature plantation of conifers within an old quarry, go right switching left to follow the wall via Coscombe Corner, to re-unite with the brink of the scarp. Follow the wall via a gate passing by the fifteen-foot high ditchless rampart of Beckbury Iron Age hill-fort to the hand-gate beside the so-called Cromwell's Monument. The statue plinth is thought to have no historic significance, but is a folly erected by the C19th owner of the Stanway estate. The route slips down through the beech clump to traverse the sheep pasture half left to a hand-gate.

Village Cross, Stanton

Elaborate gatehouse to Stanway House

MAP 5   BECKBURY *to* PUCK PIT LANE

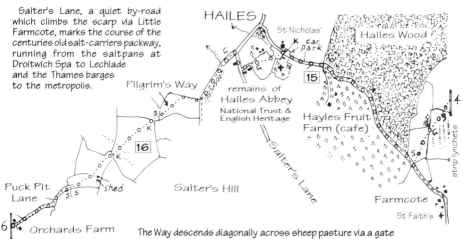

Salter's Lane, a quiet by-road which climbs the scarp via Little Farmcote, marks the course of the centuries old salt-carriers packway, running from the saltpans at Droitwich Spa to Lechlade and the Thames barges to the metropolis.

The Way descends diagonally across sheep pasture via a gate beside the spinney corner. Notice in this vicinity evidence of medieval cultivation terracing. Continue down to a stile into the Farmcote lane, go right, with frequent glimpses over Hayles Fruit Farm, lower down notice the old cobbling, worn with age. The road is then followed past the entrance to Hailes Abbey to a kissing-gate. Time spent quietly strolling around the romantic ruins of Hailes Abbey connected to the audio tape is richly rewarded. Embark upon the Pilgrim's Way, and traverse the meadow to a gate into a short lane. At Salter's Lane, go right, then left along the bridle lane via a gate. At the end of a strip of scrub woodland bear right by a light barrier, pass along the slightly sunken green way till guided half left across the arable land, aiming for the target waymark in the corner. A stile leads into a further arable field, however, the path cuts across the corner to a kissing-gate then traverses a cattle pasture. The old trod is clearly defined by the lack of thistles. The ensuing kissing-gate has all the hallmarks of an anti-backpacker device, being a trifle awkward for anyone encumbered with any sort of pack. Cross the next pasture to a ditch-hopping footway, then bear half-right down to a stile into a short fenced passage, again to thus avoiding the extremely muddy field-gate, leading into Puck Pit Lane.

Ruins of Hailes Abbey

The Pilgrim's Way from Hailes enters Winchcombe on a mischievous note. The monks appear to have been conscious of spirits, for Puck Pit meant 'the hollows where goblins lurk'. Prehaps the array of hideous gargoyles on St Peter's are a further, and later affirmation of this concern for these little discordant earth-folk.

Winchcombe lay at the centre of the Saxon king- and earldom of Mercia, with its own 'shire'. It was later home to the powerful Benedictine Abbey, described at the end of the 15th century as being equal to a little university.

With time in hand visit Sudeley Castle, a fine excuse for a day out in its own right. With other walking ideas in mind why not come back and sample either the Wychavon Way (41 miles) to the Severn at Holt Fleet, or the short Cotswold link routes, the Warden's and Windrush Ways (14 miles) which lead their separate courses to Bourton-on-the-Water.

Wadfield Roman Villa & Belas Knap.
The fragment of mosaic pavement protected within the small walled plantation is out of bounds to all walkers. This is one of several sites which flourished on the Cleeve spring-line. The Saxon name Wadfield means 'the land where woad was grown', woad being a valuable blue dye for cloth.

I would remind visitors to Belas Knap to respect its antiquity and not treat it as a picnic-cum-camp-site. It is a great pity that this important monument is so remote, exposing it to trivial abuse.

This plea has been included at the behest of English Heritage.

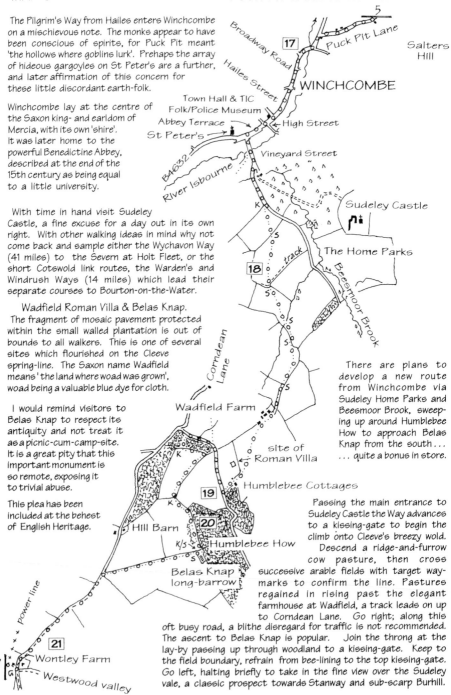

There are plans to develop a new route from Winchcombe via Sudeley Home Parks and Beesmoor Brook, sweeping up around Humblebee How to approach Belas Knap from the south... ... quite a bonus in store.

Passing the main entrance to Sudeley Castle the Way advances to a kissing-gate to begin the climb onto Cleeve's breezy wold. Descend a ridge-and-furrow cow pasture, then cross successive arable fields with target waymarks to confirm the line. Pastures regained in rising past the elegant farmhouse at Wadfield, a track leads on up to Corndean Lane. Go right; along this oft busy road, a blithe disregard for traffic is not recommended. The ascent to Belas Knap is popular. Join the throng at the lay-by passing up through woodland to a kissing-gate. Keep to the field boundary, refrain from bee-lining to the top kissing-gate. Go left, halting briefly to take in the fine view over the Sudeley vale, a classic prospect towards Stanway and sub-scarp Burhill.

St Peters' with its golden cockerel weathervane and quaint gargoyles.

MAP 7   WONTLEY FARM *to* CLEEVE HILL

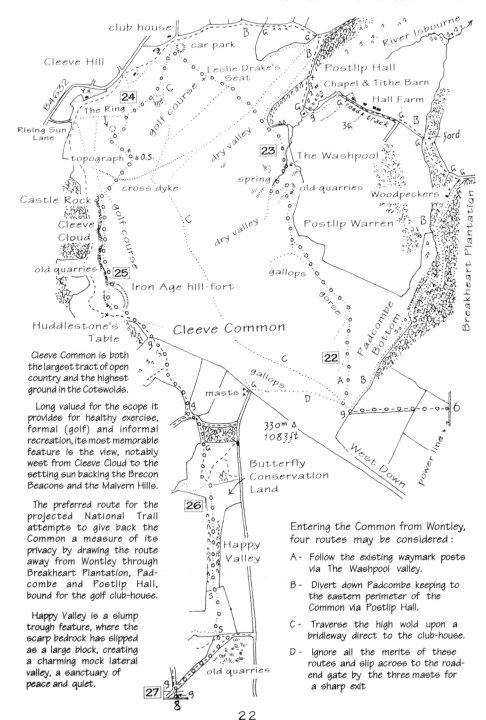

Cleeve Common is both the largest tract of open country and the highest ground in the Cotswolds.

Long valued for the scope it provides for healthy exercise, formal (golf) and informal recreation, its most memorable feature is the view, notably west from Cleeve Cloud to the setting sun backing the Brecon Beacons and the Malvern Hills.

The preferred route for the projected National Trail attempts to give back the Common a measure of its privacy by drawing the route away from Wontley through Breakheart Plantation, Padcombe and Postlip Hall, bound for the golf club-house.

Happy Valley is a slump trough feature, where the scarp bedrock has slipped as a large block, creating a charming mock lateral valley, a sanctuary of peace and quiet.

Entering the Common from Wontley, four routes may be considered:

A - Follow the existing waymark posts via The Washpool valley.

B - Divert down Padcombe keeping to the eastern perimeter of the Common via Postlip Hall.

C - Traverse the high wold upon a bridleway direct to the club-house.

D - Ignore all the merits of these routes and slip across to the road-end gate by the three masts for a sharp exit

Helen and Alison strolling
through the Happy Valley

Ascending the Wontley track a reverse glance reveals Wyck Beacon, near Stow-on-the-Wold. Entering Cleeve Common at a hand-gate, go forward, rising 100 yards, to be guided right by a series of waymark posts along sections of gallops flanked by gorse. The views are superb and on a clear day the northward vista stretches to The Wrekin in Shropshire. The path winds down into the Washpool valley. Passing the crystal spring and the silted pool, notice the unusual key-hole sheep wash. The path contours round a spur before climbing steeply up the rough pasture bank crossing tracks to wend along the fringe of the golf course through light gorse and past Leslie Drake's Seat. It was Leslie's son Tony, in chairing a local R.A. steering group, who first brought life to the concept of a long distance path the length of the Cotswold escarpment.

The Way descends to the track almost reaching the club-house (cafe), before turning south once more. Keep a keen eye on the waymark posts which can be difficult to spot in the gorse. The walk now ventures to the scarp crest and the prime viewpoints at the Rotary topograph and along the Cleeve Cloud escarpment. There are great moments to savour; the breadth of view is best appreciated with the setting sun backlighting the Black Mountains. Castle Rock is one of the soundest outcrops available to rock climbers in the Cotswolds, making it an ever popular rendezvous for budding mountaineers : in his time the author has tackled most routes, including the girdle traverse.

The Way passes through the hill-fort, departing the Common at a bridle-gate. The route descends via a further bridle-gate into a deep gully. Bear sharp left, then right, contouring below woodland, still upon a bridleway, to a gate entering to the Butterfly Reserve. Curving up to a cross-ways, continuing now as a footpath through Happy Valley, the waymark posts guide you through gorse to a stile at the southern limit of the grassland preserve. Go up left fifty yards, then right down the track, which becomes a lane approaching a road end, go left via the bridle-gates.

23

MAP 8   CLEEVE HILL to WISTLEY HILL

The bridleway meets a minor road, going left to a skew cross-roads, turn right - this stretch of road-walking provides quite a pleasant interlude.   At the left-hand bend the Way hops over a stile and continues due south through sheep pasture with the old boundary wall to the right and the memorable westward horizon of Black Mountain hills to draw the eye. Look for Blorenge and Sugar Loaf playing hide and seek behind May Hill, to the west Radnor Forest; north-west beyond the Malvern range the Abberley Hills and Titterstone Clee Hill.   Cross Ham Lane, enjoying the fine views ahead to Ravensgate Hill and Charlton Kings Common, with the outlying Robinswood and Churchdown Hills also prominent. Follow the hedge till it bears away right (polo shaped target waymark), bear slightly left down to a stile crossing Colgate Farm's private drive via stiles. The path, confined by cypress, wends down to the top of Dowdeswell Wood. Look out for the series of tree identification boards. The path keeps alongside the wood's western edge on a necessarily well drained footing. At the bottom a kissing-gate leads by a bungalow (B&B) where snacks can be obtained. Pass the small car park onto the private road which runs under the Dowdeswell Reservoir dam up to the A40. It is planned to create a new path through the grounds of the Reservoir Inn to reduce the roadside walk, however, for the present follow the footway left to the track right, and cross the busy road with the utmost care. Crossing the old railway the Way now climbs largely upon Woodland Trust land. Gaining height the path reaches a stile and is thereafter confined climbing along the edge of Lineover Wood and emerging at a stile into pasture.   Follow the hedge up to where the pasture funnels towards a stile.

   You may notice a stile in the fence to the left, some seventy yards earlier, this gains access to a spinney wherein stand three old coppiced beech trees, the lowest being the second largest beech tree in Britain, with a 24 foot girth - the largest is to be found in Ireland. Reaching the stile at the top, beside a padlocked gate turn right advancing for a further sevety yards to a stile and gate to enter Lineover Wood. Keep straight ahead to pass the massed growth of a coppiced large-leaved lime tree. The path descends to run alongside a recently laid hedge above a pasture, the woods are managed by local volunteers of the Woodland Trust who make a point of not burning any timber, hence the neat piles and brush-wood swathes. The wood-name Lineover means 'lime tree bank', confirming this to be an ancient preserve of this now rare sub-speicies which can grow to a height of 150 feet making it the tallest native tree in Britain.. The path winds down to a stile to enter a cattle pasture, from where the footpath climbs directly passing a waymark post to find a weighted hand-gate in the top corner. The path runs along the foot of the scarp bank, then climbs upon a thin steep trod. At the top pause and glance back over the valley to Cleeve Cloud, along the line of our route. Now walk through the Plantation via the gate and on along the open track to the main road.

Cleeve Common across the Chelt Valley from Ravensgate Hill

Cheltenham Park Hotel

MAP 9   WISTLEY HILL *to* CHARLTON KINGS COMMON

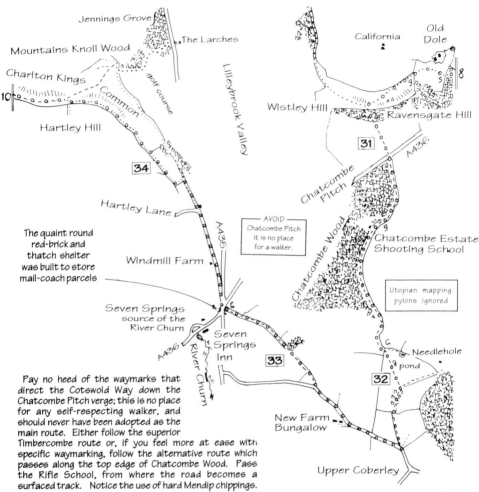

The quaint round red-brick and thatch shelter was built to store mail-coach parcels

Pay no heed of the waymarks that direct the Cotswold Way down the Chatcombe Pitch verge; this is no place for any self-respecting walker, and should never have been adopted as the main route. Either follow the superior Timbercombe route or, if you feel more at ease with specific waymarking, follow the alternative route which passes along the top edge of Chatcombe Wood. Pass the Rifle School, from where the road becomes a surfaced track. Notice the use of hard Mendip chippings.

Reaching a gate, head diagonally right across the field, glancing past a mid-course pond, aiming for the target waymark disc (in a former life a road speed limit sign). Go right, in a light surround of trees, then alongside the old hedge on the left, passing through a gateway now with the hedge to the right to meet the open road at Upper Coberley (pronounced Cubbalee). Go right, taking the waymarked track bearing right, which leads down the dry valley past a pheasant cover to Seven Springs. Gingerly negotiate the broad road junction. Close at hand the source of the River Churn is of interest. Being the furthest point of any headwater from London Bridge, one could pronounce this the true source of the Thames, the Latin inscription on site adding fuel to this outrageous proposition. If there be time for debate then do so in the Seven Springs Inn, with pint in hand. Whilst musing on the little river consider its name, fashioned from Celtic, and adopted by the Romans in their town-name Corinium.

Follow Hartley Lane to the sharp left bend, continuing on the footpath (used as if a bridleway hence the duck-boards). Bearing left under the initial canopy of rank hedge, follow the underside of a hedge, then wall, onto Charlton Kings Common, via a couple of anti-rider barriers. The views just keep getting better with every stride, over the Lilleybrook valley to Cleeve Hill, Cheltenham and the broadening vale to the Malvern Hills. The popularity of this parade is quite understandable.

The preferred National Trail route will leave the A435 through the car park of the Lilley Brook Golf Club glancing to the north of Jennings Grove before linking to the current path, round the south flank of Mountains Knoll Wood, then up the old trackway onto the common, a steady 550 foot ascent.

Ravensgate Hill from Wistley Hill

Mountains Knoll Wood and Lilleybrook Golf Course from Charlton Kings Common

MAP 10   CHARLTON KINGS COMMON to BIRDLIP

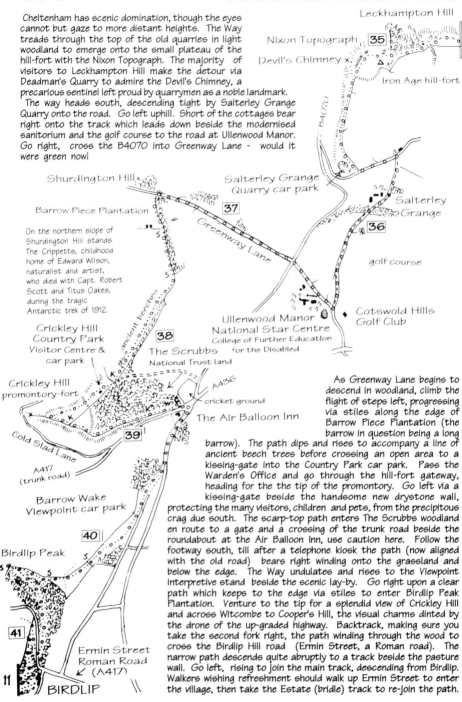

Cheltenham has scenic domination, though the eyes cannot but gaze to more distant heights. The Way treads through the top of the old quarries in light woodland to emerge onto the small plateau of the hill-fort with the Nixon Topograph. The majority of visitors to Leckhampton Hill make the detour via Deadman's Quarry to admire the Devil's Chimney, a precarious sentinel left proud by quarrymen as a noble landmark.

The way heads south, descending tight by Salterley Grange Quarry onto the road. Go left uphill. Short of the cottages bear right onto the track which leads down beside the modernised sanitorium and the golf course to the road at Ullenwood Manor. Go right, cross the B4070 into Greenway Lane - would it were green now!

Leckhampton Hill

Nixon Topograph 35

Devil's Chimney ×

Iron Age hill-fort

Shurdington Hill

Salterley Grange Quarry car park

Barrow Piece Plantation

37

Greenway Lane

Salterley Grange

36

golf course

On the northern slope of Shurdington Hill stands The Crippetts, childhood home of Edward Wilson, naturalist and artist, who died with Capt. Robert Scott and Titus Oakes, during the tragic Antarctic trek of 1912.

Crickley Hill Country Park
Visitor Centre & car park

38

The Scrubbs
National Trust land

Ullenwood Manor
National Star Centre
College of Further Education for the Disabled

Cotswold Hills Golf Club

Crickley Hill promontory-fort

A436

39

cricket ground

The Air Balloon Inn

Cold Slad Lane

A417 (trunk road)

Barrow Wake Viewpoint car park

40

Birdlip Peak

41

Ermin Street Roman Road (A417)

11

BIRDLIP

As Greenway Lane begins to descend in woodland, climb the flight of steps left, progressing via stiles along the edge of Barrow Piece Plantation (the barrow in question being a long barrow). The path dips and rises to accompany a line of ancient beech trees before crossing an open area to a kissing-gate into the Country Park car park. Pass the Warden's Office and go through the hill-fort gateway, heading for the the tip of the promontory. Go left via a kissing-gate beside the handsome new drystone wall, protecting the many visitors, children and pets, from the precipitous crag due south. The scarp-top path enters The Scrubbs woodland en route to a gate and a crossing of the trunk road beside the roundabout at the Air Balloon Inn, use caution here. Follow the footway south, till after a telephone kiosk the path (now aligned with the old road) bears right winding onto the grassland and below the edge. The Way undulates and rises to the Viewpoint interpretive stand beside the scenic lay-by. Go right upon a clear path which keeps to the edge via stiles to enter Birdlip Peak Plantation. Venture to the tip for a splendid view of Crickley Hill and across Witcombe to Cooper's Hill, the visual charms dinted by the drone of the up-graded highway. Backtrack, making sure you take the second fork right, the path winding through the wood to cross the Birdlip Hill road (Ermin Street, a Roman road). The narrow path descends quite abruptly to a track beside the pasture wall. Go left, rising to join the main track, descending from Birdlip. Walkers wishing refreshment should walk up Ermin Street to enter the village, then take the Estate (bridle) track to re-join the path.

(above) The inviting winding trail leading south from the Barrow Wake Viewpoint bound for Birdlip Peak. In the distance across Witcombe are Cooper's Hill and Robinswood Hill.

(below) The crag-lined Crickley Hill and Scrubbs Wood from the same location.

MAP 11   BIRDLIP to COOPER'S HILL

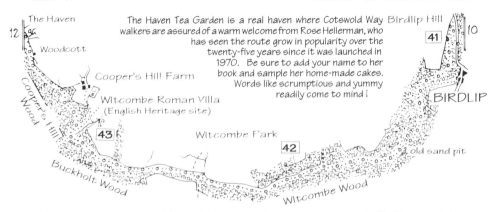

The Haven Tea Garden is a real haven where Cotswold Way walkers are assured of a warm welcome from Rose Hellerman, who has seen the route grow in popularity over the twenty-five years since it was launched in 1970. Be sure to add your name to her book and sample her home-made cakes. Words like scrumptious and yummy readily come to mind !

The main track running through Witcombe Woods, vechicular access exclusive to the Witcombe Estate, is infrequently muddy and gives a simple-to-adhere-to line through the managed woodlands. The numerous branching tracks and paths are no distraction to the waymarked route. The group of old reservoirs in the vale below also belong to the Witcombe Park estate. Known as Witcombe Waters, they are an angler's delight, having been pensioned off from domestic supply when the aluminium content became unacceptably high. Walkers are encouraged to make the short detour to inspect the remains of Witcombe Roman Villa; a track leads down and out of the wood. The complex site is presently deficient of the necessary interpretative boards, but plans are afoot to remedy this. Remarkably the sloping site has lost little of its sylvan beauty down nearly two millenia, the background drone of the new Crickley Hill road is the one unfortunate addition to the otherwise peaceful experience back down this mental time-path.

Helen   tracking   through   Witcombe   Wood

Churchdown Hill from the top of the Cheese-rolling slope on Cooper's Hill Common.

MAP 12   COOPER'S HILL to PAINSWICK

Leave the road at Stoneleigh entering the car parking area below the precipitous Cheese Roling slope. A path winds up from the kissing-gate to the flag-pole, a fine spot to rest and ponder on the spacious view to Gloucester Cathedral and the Cotswold scarp to Bredon and Cleeve. Head south-west upon Cooper's Hill Common (Local Nature Reserve) and follow the path forking right. This descends in woodland, pass over a bridle-path, turning left after just a few paces at the path junction. The path dips through a wet depression to exit Brockworth Wood via a short hedged passage between pastures. Bear left, keeping to the upper edge of Upton Wood. The path sweeps uphill cresting the shoulder of High Brotheridge where an English Nature sign heralds entry into a section of Buckholt Wood. Keep right, descending close to the old wall to meet the road at Cranham Corner. Go right to the bus shelter and cross the A46, then go left entering the wood right on a path accompanying the wall bounding Prinknash Park. Watch for the left turn; opposite a wall-stile, cross the Upton road via a car park, advancing through this detached portion of Buckholt Wood on Kite's Hill.

44

Cooper's Hill
Cheese Rolling Slope

The Haven

Brockworth Wood

Cooper's Wood

11

Fiddler's Elbow car park

Upton Wood

Prinknash Abbey

High Brotheridge

45

earthworks of British settlement

Rough Park

Buckholt Wood

Prinknash Park

Cranham Corner

Kite's Hill

Pope's Wood

46

Royal William Hotel

Castle Lodge

Kimsbury Iron Age hill-fort

Painswick Beacon

golf course

47 Catbrain Quarry

golf course

club house

cemetery

B4073

A46

Painswick House

Golf Course Road

Advancing through old coppice woodland to join a by-road, passing Castle Lodge, the track forks. Go forward by the gate onto Painswick Hill, keeping to the open trackway running between golf fairways, then light pine woodland, amongst old quarrying.

If you would like to include the summit of Painswick Beacon follow the track beside Pope's Wood bearing half-left along the quarried edge of the ramparts to the O.S. column. The panorama is immensely rewarding embracing the broad Severn vale with Robinswood Hill in the near ground, backed by the Forest of Dean and the distant three peaks of Abergavenny, the beech-clothed scarplands to the north-east, and to the south the Haresfield Beacon spur. Re-join the waymarked route by carefully descending the eroded ramparts keeping to the western fringe of woodland.

Upon reaching the open cross ridge road, the Way goes left and right at the millstone along the access track to Catbrain Quarry. Keep left by the limestone blocks at the entrance, pursuing a narrow path contouring through woodland. When this breaks out, look left for any golfers preparing to tee-off from the club-house below; a half hit stroke may alight heavily on your head ! Advance to the top of the cemetery following the wall before next crossing another unenclosed road. Maintaining course to reach Golf Course Road, go right to its junction with the B4073. Go left to enter the charming village of Painswick.

13

Saltridge Wood beyond Painswick Hill golf club-house

MAP 13   PAINSWICK to STOCKEND WOOD

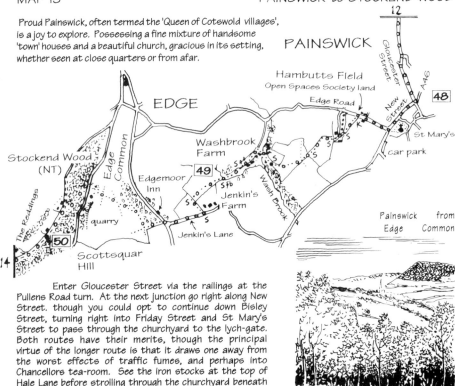

Proud Painswick, often termed the 'Queen of Cotswold villages', is a joy to explore. Possessing a fine mixture of handsome 'town' houses and a beautiful church, gracious in its setting, whether seen at close quarters or from afar.

PAINSWICK

Painswick from Edge Common

Enter Gloucester Street via the railings at the Pullens Road turn. At the next junction go right along New Street. though you could opt to continue down Bisley Street, turning right into Friday Street and St Mary's Street to pass through the churchyard to the lych-gate. Both routes have their merits, though the principal virtue of the longer route is that it draws one away from the worst effects of traffic fumes, and perhaps into Chancellors tea-room. See the iron stocks at the top of Hale Lane before strolling through the churchyard beneath yew avenues and past an array of classical C17th table and tea-caddy tombs. Reputedly there are never more than ninety-nine yews, though as many are looking decidedly long in the limb, a re-planting scheme may well be soon due.

Turn right opposite the lych-gate along Edge Road. After Hambutts Mead go left via the kissing-gate/stile down Hambutts Field, the property of the Open Spaces Society. The long seat may appeal as a spot for a rambling group picnic. Where the field tapers, cross the stile and pass between gardens to emerge at a stile with a fine view over the Washbrook valley to Edge Common. Follow the right-hand fence downhill to a stile, continue beside the left-hand hedge which shields tennis courts, until directed half-right to a white disc target waymark in a projecting hedge corner. Keep beside the hedge to a stile in the corner. The footpath runs beside a fence and above the obscured stream, descending to a gate behind Washbrook Farm, an old mill, crossing the brook pass beyond the house. Keep round by the outbuildings (rather than follow the drive which is signed 'Painswick, Edge Road') upon the gravel track. The path leads past two large corrugated sheds, and soon rises to a stile in the fence on the left. Follow the narrow pasture shelf right, to a stile into the wooded surrounds of a small stream, advance to a footbridge and stile rising into an old orchard pasture. Ascend directly to a stile in the fence, do not be lured to tread the muddy way of the dairy cattle on the left, but follow the fence and subsequent hedge above Jenkin's Farm to a squeeze stile onto the road, Jenkin's Lane. Go right, uphill to the junction.

The Edgemoor Inn, close at hand to the right, may proove irresistible on a hot day, and why not! The Way crosses directly over the A4173 into the confined path rising beside a wall. Continue a few paces beyond the wall-end, before turning right and pursuing a level path with old quarrying to the right and light birchwood on either hand. Watch for the waymark post guiding left up the ancient pasture of Edge Common. The path winds uphill over two transverse tracks with spacious views, notably east towards Painswick and its backing of beechwoods. At the top of the Common, enter Scottsquar Quarry. Waymark posts guide left to a short flight of rough-cut rock-steps and metal hand-rail leading through light woodland and up to the road. Go straight across by the bus stop, descending into Stockend Wood. Reaching a track at the foot of the slope, go left. Pass The Reddings, a novel hexagonal cottage with recent cottage extension, in a most attractive setting.

Painswick Post Office

Stockend Wood

MAP 14   STOCKEND WOOD to DOVEROW HILL

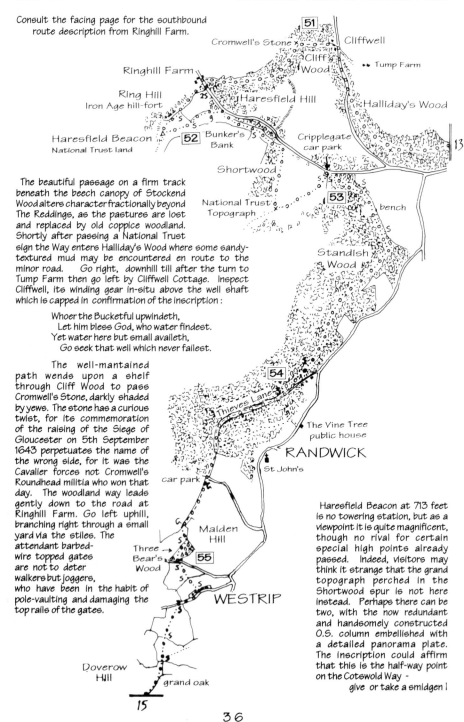

Consult the facing page for the southbound
route description from Ringhill Farm.

Cromwell's Stone
Cliffwell
Cliff
Wood
Tump Farm
Ringhill Farm
Ring Hill
Iron Age hill-fort
Haresfield Hill
Halliday's Wood
Haresfield Beacon
National Trust land
Bunker's
Bank
Cripplegate
car park
13
Shortwood
National Trust
Topograph
bench
Standish
Wood
Thieves Lane
The Vine Tree
public house
RANDWICK
St John's
car park
Malden
Hill
Three →
Bear's
Wood
WESTRIP
Doverow
Hill
grand oak
15
51
52
53
54
55

The beautiful passage on a firm track
beneath the beech canopy of Stockend
Wood alters character fractionally beyond
The Reddings, as the pastures are lost
and replaced by old coppice woodland.
Shortly after passing a National Trust
sign the Way enters Halliday's Wood where some sandy-
textured mud may be encountered en route to the
minor road.   Go right, downhill till after the turn to
Tump Farm then go left by Cliffwell Cottage. Inspect
Cliffwell, its winding gear in-situ above the well shaft
which is capped in confirmation of the inscription :

> Whoer the Bucketful upwindeth,
>   Let him bless God, who water findest.
> Yet water here but small availeth,
>   Go seek that well which never failest.

The well-mantained
path wends upon a shelf
through Cliff Wood to pass
Cromwell's Stone, darkly shaded
by yews. The stone has a curious
twist, for its commemoration
of the raising of the Siege of
Gloucester on 5th September
1643 perpetuates the name of
the wrong side, for it was the
Cavalier forces not Cromwell's
Roundhead militia who won that
day.   The woodland way leads
gently down to the road at
Ringhill Farm. Go left uphill,
branching right through a small
yard via the stiles. The
attendant barbed-
wire topped gates
are not to deter
walkers but joggers,
who have been in the habit of
pole-vaulting and damaging the
top rails of the gates.

Haresfield Beacon at 713 feet
is no towering station, but as a
viewpoint it is quite magnificent,
though no rival for certain
special high points already
passed. Indeed, visitors may
think it strange that the grand
topograph perched in the
Shortwood spur is not here
instead. Perhaps there can be
two, with the now redundant
and handsomely constructed
O.S. column embellished with
a detailed panorama plate.
The inscription could affirm
that this is the half-way point
on the Cotswold Way -
give or take a smidgen !

Cliff Well
(left)

(below) Redundant O.S. column
on Haresfield Beacon

From Ringhill Farm the Way ascends a green track inclining to the edge. Keep to the outside of the fence leading to a stile entering the hill-fort enclosure. Advance beside the shallow ramparts, slipping through the old quarry to the stone column at the tip of Haresfield Beacon.
Backtrack along the southern rampart with further fine views over the combe to Bunker's Bank, Haresfield Hill and the Shortwood spur, our next objective. Passing through a squeeze stile, the path is once more confined by a fence to the left in heading for a wall-stile from where the path leads pleasantly to the road and lay-by car parking area. The Way steps not a stride upon the highway, instead departs down the steps below the National Trust contributory box, bearing left to pursue a path beneath the wall and along the head of the combe accompanied by a fence via a stile before climbing through woodland on a broad path onto the Shortwood spur. Bear right along the pasture to reach the topograph with its generous views, being not so hindered by trees as the recently departed Beacon viewpoint.
Head back north-east to pass through the Cripplegate car park via squeeze stiles, thereby avoiding the road, to enter the upper portion of Standish Wood on a level path. Proceed via further stiles and one splendid woodland breach viewpoint. Shortly after the second stile, come to a path junction and bear right amid the coppiced rows. Keep to the main path where it trends down the ridge, passing a notice advising of the availability of a National Trust camping ground. The path draws into Thieves Lane entered at a stile.   Go right.   Should refreshment be a consideration then divergent paths offer the opportunity of diverting to The Vine Tree in Randwick.
The lane emerges into a road with adjacent car park. Go straight on via the gate, now with a wall to the right follow the ridge to a short lane and gate, and veer half-left at the lane end to a stone stile into Three Bears Wood (check porridge, chair and bed!).   At the foot, pass left down the road for a few yards to where a stile guides the Way down a pasture to another stile.   Descend the bank to a narrow passage beside cottages to emerge on the lane in Westrip. Go right, until again guided left via a stile and down the pastures.   Note the metal squeeze stile characteristic of the Stroud locality, at the bottom a wet gateway has been alleviated by provision of a brick path for walkers. Subsequently, rise beside the hedge passing under a large oak, keeping the hedge to the left in crossing the shoulder of Doverow Hill.

37

MAP 15   DOVEROW HILL to STANLEY WOOD

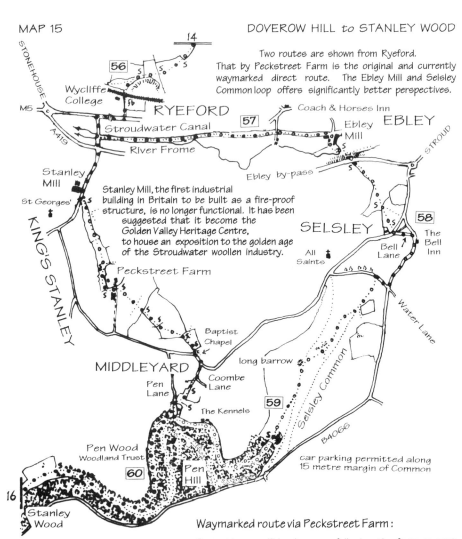

Two routes are shown from Ryeford. That by Peckstreet Farm is the original and currently waymarked direct route. The Ebley Mill and Selsley Common loop offers significantly better perspectives.

Stanley Mill, the first industrial building in Britain to be built as a fire-proof structure, is no longer functional. It has been suggested that it become the Golden Valley Heritage Centre, to house an exposition to the golden age of the Stroudwater woollen industry.

car parking permitted along 15 metre margin of Common

Waymarked route via Peckstreet Farm:

Cross the new Ebley by-pass, following the footway past Stanley Mill, bearing left almost opposite Stanley House by a short lane and cottage to a stile. A level green way leads via a gateway to a stile just short of the farm. Keeping the shallow valley on the right, pass via the rough pasture to the garden corner stile. Follow the willows left to the access road, and go over via the stile to traverse the arable field half-right. From the next stile advance with a hedge to the right crossing a stile in a shortened length of fence, before angling half-left to a stile beside back garden fencing, which is accompanied by a squeeze stile into a short lane past King's Stanley Baptist Chapel, onto the road in Middleyard. Go left to Rosebank Cattery, turning right up Coombe Lane. As the lane bends left, go right up the confined footpath beside an orchard to a neatly stepped stile. Passing a brief thicket, bear uphill to the top corner of the pasture squeeze stile into Pen Lane. Continue the ascent left between the cottages Brushwood and The Penn. The metalled road replaced by a narrow lane. The rocky footing is slippery when wet.

At the top of Pen Lane keep right beside the fence, contouring through a delightful beech-wood curving round the combe. After a divergent Woodland Trust stepped path, the Way descends, becoming muddier in shaggier woodland, weaving through an area of bracken and bramble to reach a stile into cow pasture. Contouring forward, it gradually comes close under Stanley Wood amid more bracken and bramble.

Ebley Mill

Selsley Common route:

Follow the canal towpath from Spring Cottages soon, mesopotamian fashion, runs between the Stroudwater Canal and the River Frome. The river slips away right as the path rises by Double Locks Cottage. After the open lock only reeds linger within the canal basin. Approaching the Bridge Road crossing, the canal is so infilled that a track has requisitioned its course. Soon the handsome brick form of Ebley Mill looms ahead and the path ventures onto the concrete roadway (upon the canal's course) going beneath Greenaway's canopy to meet the roadway to Stroud District Council's Ebley Mill offices. Go right, admiring the mill's imposing stature. Pass the new council chambers, bear left through the car park to Meadow Lodge, crossing the Frome bridge to a squeeze stile. Advance through the meadow to the blue-brick underpass of the old railway embankment to cross the Ebley by-pass to a stile. Ascend the parkland cattle pasture beside the fence, angling half-left from the dead Scot's pine across two hollows to a squeeze stile beside a gateway in the metal fencing. Continue up the slope to a squeeze stile in the roadside wall to enter the village of Selsley. Cross into Bell Lane, and at the next junction follow the footway right, passing The Bell Inn. Notice the novel pottery parish map on the pub wall, created to mark the Queen's Silver Jubilee in 1977.

Rise above the village, passing through the hand-gate beside the cattle-grid access to Selsley Common. Opposite Water Lane go right up the minor road. At its brow bear left up the green track, passing the barrier rising to a wall corner where the path bears right up the hollow-way with excellent reverse views over Stroud and up the Painswick valley to Painswick Beacon. Where it forks after 30 yards, keep to the hollow-way, and at the next fork hold to the shallow left-hand hollow-way following the edge around an old quarried area to reach the long barrow viewpoint. The view stretches from the Malborough Downs in the south-east to Pen-y-fan to the west. Notice below the Austrian Tyrol-styled saddleback tower of All Saints Church - replicated by Ebley Mill. The footpath leads south from the barrow, drifting gently diagonally down the slope, passing close under an old quarry to reach a stile entry into Pen Wood (with welcoming Woodland Trust sign). A firm path descends through the beechwood, gaining gradient to join a level track, go left after rain a muddy way. At the point where a descending track cuts across to The Kennels, descending as a very steep tarmac roadway, continue forward above the cottage on a green path, soon accompanying the pastureside fence. Shortly, this twists briefly up left, regaining the fence to emerge at the top of Pen Lane.

MAP 16   STANLEY WOOD to CAM LONG DOWN

Re-enter the woodland at the top corner of the pasture. Climbing steadily through the beechwood, cross a diagonal track to reach the rim of an old quarry protected by a fence. After a pole barrier, cross a further diagonal track, the path continues along the scarp edge until accompanied by a fence close to the main road. Arriving at the path junction, near the road, bear half-right, then turn left up the steps beside a fence, again protecting an old quarry brink, to slip through a barrier into the 12-acre Coaley Peak Country Park. Cross the grassland site road venturing up to inspect the exposed interior of Nympsfield long barrow. Thirteen skeletons were exhumed from the gallery during the excavation of 1937. These and various small personal artefacts dating from about 2500 B.C. are held by Stroud Museum.

Pass in front of the car park along the scarp-top fence, revelling in the grand views across the lias clay vale to Slimbridge, home of the Wildfowl Trust's New Grounds reserve beside The Noose, a broad tidal reach of the River Severn. From the kissing-gate, enter National Trust land and descend to the scenically strategic Topograph.

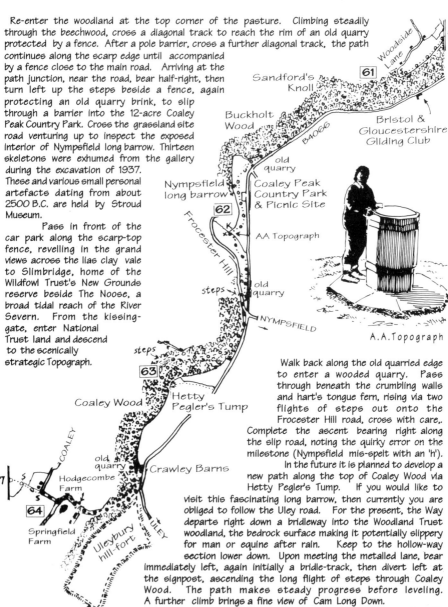

Sandford's Knoll

Buckholt Wood

Bristol & Gloucestershire Gliding Club

old quarry

Nympsfield long barrow

Coaley Peak Country Park & Picnic Site

Frocester Hill

AA Topograph

steps

old quarry

NYMPSFIELD

A.A.Topograph

Woodside Lane

15

61

B4066

62

63

Hetty Pegler's Tump

Coaley Wood

steps

old quarry

Crawley Barns

COALEY

Hodgecombe Farm

17

64

Springfield Farm

Uleybury hill-fort

ULEY

Walk back along the old quarried edge to enter a wooded quarry. Pass through beneath the crumbling walls and hart's tongue fern, rising via two flights of steps out onto the Frocester Hill road, cross with care. Complete the ascent bearing right along the slip road, noting the quirky error on the milestone (Nympsfield mis-spelt with an 'h').

In the future it is planned to develop a new path along the top of Coaley Wood via Hetty Pegler's Tump. If you would like to visit this fascinating long barrow, then currently you are obliged to follow the Uley road. For the present, the Way departs right down a bridleway into the Woodland Trust woodland, the bedrock surface making it potentially slippery for man or equine after rain. Keep to the hollow-way section lower down. Upon meeting the metalled lane, bear immediately left, again initially a bridle-track, then divert left at the signpost, ascending the long flight of steps through Coaley Wood. The path makes steady progress before leveling. A further climb brings a fine view of Cam Long Down.

It is planned to bring the new path down to re-unite with the existing route, prior to the old quarry. Beyond the quarry the path passes barriers and merges with an ascending track. At the brow, bear right down a bridleway which runs diagonally down the slope of Uleybury. A circuit of Uleybury, the 32-acre Iron Age hill-fort, is highly recommended, a green bridle-track accomplishing the entire orbit upon a rampart terrace. The bridleway leading down to Springfield Farm switches from bedrock, to sand, to sticky ankle-deep clay in the bottom hollow-way. Follow the drive to the minor road, go right, and at the bend take the stile to the left. Keep the ascending hedge to the right, to reach a stile into the steep sheep pasture of Cam Long Down.

The Tableland
from Coaley Peak

River Severn
(The Noose)

Forest of
Dean

May
Hill

The
Woolhope
Hills

Looking   north-west   from   Coaley   Peak

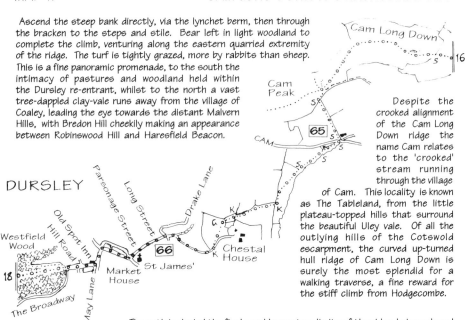

Ascend the steep bank directly, via the lynchet berm, then through the bracken to the steps and stile. Bear left in light woodland to complete the climb, venturing along the eastern quarried extremity of the ridge. The turf is tightly grazed, more by rabbits than sheep. This is a fine panoramic promenade, to the south the intimacy of pastures and woodland held within the Dursley re-entrant, whilst to the north a vast tree-dappled clay-vale runs away from the village of Coaley, leading the eye towards the distant Malvern Hills, with Bredon Hill cheekily making an appearance between Robinswood Hill and Haresfield Beacon.

Despite the crooked alignment of the Cam Long Down ridge the name Cam relates to the 'crooked' stream running through the village of Cam. This locality is known as The Tableland, from the little plateau-topped hills that surround the beautiful Uley vale. Of all the outlying hills of the Cotswold escarpment, the curved up-turned hull ridge of Cam Long Down is surely the most splendid for a walking traverse, a fine reward for the stiff climb from Hodgecombe.

The path is denied the final scrubby western limits of the ridge, being ushered left down a diagonal rutted path to the depression below Cam Peak, at the bend in an ancient hollow-way. Currently the Cotswold Way is waymarked over the little crest of Cam Peak (Peaked Down on O.S. maps) through the bracken, but the better and future route of the Way takes the righthand of two paths bearing left from the saddle leading through the bracken. Keep right to a stile in the fence/old hazel hedge. Descend the sheep pasture with the hedge to the left to a stile onto the road, go right then left through the squeeze stile onto the plank passage and along the narrow path beside the gullied stream. Pass a cottage garden, cross a stile into cow pasture, continue straight ahead rising up the slope to accompany the fence left to a metal kissing-gate. Proceed with the fence to the right and subsequent hedge to a kissing-gate. Continue to

a gate then bear half-left between the holm oak and the dead redwood, descending alongside the fence to a kissing-gate entry into the drive from The Chestal. Incidentally, this unusual name derives from the Saxon and meant either a gravelly place, or was indicative of evidence of Roman ruins.

The Market House

Go right down to the lodge, re-joining the existing Cotswold Way, adjacent to a Bowls Club. Bear left along Chestal Lane, then ascend Long Street into the centre of Dursley. Dursley, known more for its association with Lister Engineering and Bailey's Newspapers than for its obvious charm, grew up as a major centre of cottage-industry to the cloth trade.

Reaching the busy junction notice the handsome brick facade of Lloyd's Bank and the Market House ahead, cross into pedestrian Parsonage Street. At the end of this principal shopping street, go left along May Lane and passing the bus station, bear right at the Old Spot Inn (a cosy little pub) ascending the 14% gradient of Hill Road. At the bend go forward past the chain, taking the left, rising, track on a steady climb through Cockshoot Wood to Stinchcombe Hill.

Coaley Peak from Cam Long Down

Drakestone Point from across Hollow Combe

43

MAP 18   STINCHCOMBE HILL to BRACKENBURY DITCHES

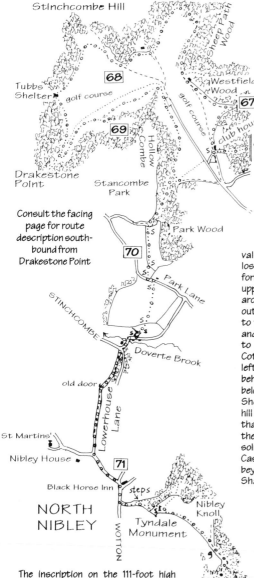

Stinchcombe Hill

Tubbs Shelter

golf course

68

69

Hollow Combe

Drakestone Point

Stancombe Park

Sheep Path Wood

Westfield Wood

67

golf course

club house

17

S

Consult the facing page for route description south-bound from Drakestone Point

Park Wood

S

70

S

S

Park Lane

STINCHCOMBE

S

S

Doverte Brook

old door

St Martins'

Nibley House

Lowerhouse Lane

71

Black Horse Inn   steps

NORTH NIBLEY

WOTTON

Tyndale Monument

Nibley Knoll

Westridge Wood

National Trust land

72

Brackenbury Ditches hill-fort

19

The inscription on the 111-foot high Tyndale Monument reads :

'Erected A.D. 1866 in grateful remembrance of William Tyndale, translator of the English Bible who first caused the New Testament to be printed in the mother tongue of his countrymen; born near this spot, he suffered martyrdom at Vilvorde in Flanders on 6th October 1536'.

Confined by garden fencing at its culmination, the path emerges from the wood at twin squeeze stiles right beside Dursley Golf Club. Walkers in a hurry can cut across the neck of the ridge, but the grand 2½ mile tour of Stinchcombe Hill has everything to commend it. The complete circuit is described, so ignore the Cotswold Way waymarking directing you onto the roadway.

Go right in front of the club-house, diverting off the metalled sur-face, to accompany the path curving right along the outside edge of the trees. As the open ground funnels, bear sharp left, maintaining company with the path along the outside of the woodland. Passing the maintenance sheds, and follow the bridleway into the top fringe of Sheep Path Wood. Enjoy momentary vistas over the Dursley vale to Uleybury and Coaley Peak. Without losing height come back out of the woodland, forking right and passing a seat. Keep to the upper path curving again within light woodland around the perimeter of the golf course, coming out onto grassland rough with fine views across to the Severn. Cross the path signed 'Woodfield' and its unenclosed house drive, following the wall to join a bridle-track, the currently waymarked Cotswold Way. Where this begins to descend, cut left across the front of the 12th tee, and keep behind the next corner tee, the path now running below the general level of the fairway to the Tubbs Shelter. Sir Stanley Tubbs bequeathed the hill to the public forever in 1930 and it is fitting that a moment be spent at this spot, though the M5 motorway ensures it will not be a silent solitude. The westward view features Berkeley Castle three miles distant as the crow flies, beyond the de-commissioned power station and Sharpness Docks facing Lydney across the Severn shore. Hidden below is the village of Stinchcombe, the place-name derived from 'valley of the sandpiper'.

The edge path now ventures up past the topograph, the white-washed O.S. column at 719 feet, and on past the stone memorial seat to slip through the four narrow ramparts to a metal seat at the furthest tip of Drakestone Point. which means 'dragon's headland'.

44

Hollow Combe and Nibley Knoll from Stinchcombe Hill

Drakestone Point is a most pleasant viewpoint looking south over Stancombe to Nibley Knoll and Brackenbury Ditches, with the distant diminishing scarp leading the eye to Dyrham and Little Down. Backtrack only a few paces before slipping down through the remnant thicket right on a path that contours below the curving edge to rise onto the intermediate spur. Approaching the seat, bear left back into light woodland to curve above a precipitious grassland slope. Reaching the head of Hollow Combe admire the view towards Nibley Knoll, a most satisfying scarpland prospect.

Continue round, and slightly up, to pass along the edge of woodland once more till just after the 2nd tee where the Way departs right into the woodland. Descending a short way to join a bridleway, continue left downhill. Coming to the edge of farmland, leave the trackway left, slipping through a hollow-way via steps beside black gas pipes to reach a stile into cow pasture. Proceed with the fence to the right, ignore the first stile, cross the stile where the fence kinks left, and descend to a stile onto the Park Lane road. Go left, and after Park Farm House, go right over the stile descending the pasture along the ghost alignment of an old hedge to another stile. Continue down the steepening slope to a stile into a small tapering enclosure to a stile onto the road. Go right past a brick cottage, crossing Doverte Brook, rising to the junction. Cross the road, alert to speeding traffic, particularly from the blind lefthand bend. Ascend Lowerhouse Lane, glancing at the curious old door with datestone 1607.

This charming lane enters North Nibley bearing left along The Street to the road junction opposite the Black Horse Inn. Go right, beyond the kiosk, then go left into the sunken lane. Read the notice with advice on obtaining a key to the Tyndale Monument (either from the village stores or close by at Knoyle House - deposit £2, adults 50p, children 20p). Ascend the lane to branch right up the cleverly engineered steps up the wooded bank to a squeeze stile access to Nibley Knoll. William Tyndale, reputedly born in North Nibley in 1484, was a remarkably brave man, his translation a masterpiece of literary inspiration.

Pass the Silver Jubilee topograph block, following the fence-line with views into Waterley Bottom, to enter Westridge Wood at a hand-gate. Bear right at the radial path junction, forking left along the bridleway through coppiced and larch woodland. The path curves left beside the hill-fort ramparts shortly after the ditch drifts away a path joins from the right. In beechwood cross an ascending path, continue along the edge, in due course running adjacent to arable land.

45

MAP 19   BRACKENBURY DITCHES *to* KILCOTT MILL

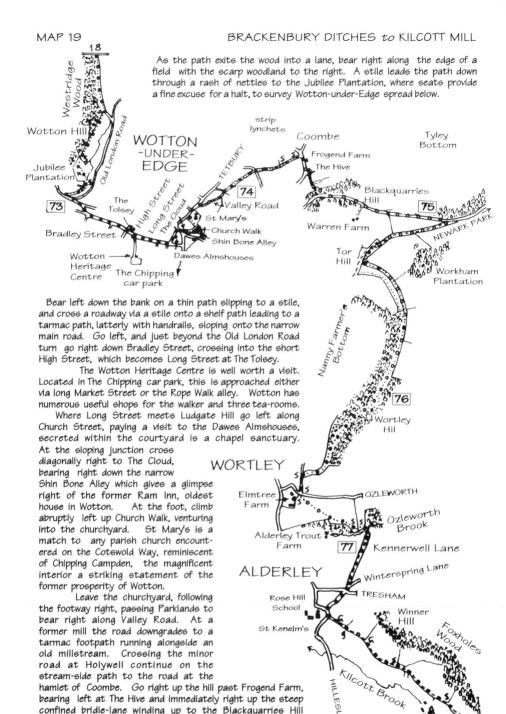

As the path exits the wood into a lane, bear right along the edge of a field with the scarp woodland to the right. A stile leads the path down through a rash of nettles to the Jubilee Plantation, where seats provide a fine excuse for a halt, to survey Wotton-under-Edge spread below.

Bear left down the bank on a thin path slipping to a stile, and cross a roadway via a stile onto a shelf path leading to a tarmac path, latterly with handrails, sloping onto the narrow main road. Go left, and just beyond the Old London Road turn go right down Bradley Street, crossing into the short High Street, which becomes Long Street at The Tolsey.

The Wotton Heritage Centre is well worth a visit. Located in The Chipping car park, this is approached either via long Market Street or the Rope Walk alley. Wotton has numerous useful shops for the walker and three tea-rooms.

Where Long Street meets Ludgate Hill go left along Church Street, paying a visit to the Dawes Almshouses, secreted within the courtyard is a chapel sanctuary. At the sloping junction cross diagonally right to The Cloud, bearing right down the narrow Shin Bone Alley which gives a glimpse right of the former Ram Inn, oldest house in Wotton. At the foot, climb abruptly left up Church Walk, venturing into the churchyard. St Mary's is a match to any parish church encountered on the Cotswold Way, reminiscent of Chipping Campden, the magnificent interior a striking statement of the former prosperity of Wotton.

Leave the churchyard, following the footway right, passing Parklands to bear right along Valley Road. At a former mill the road downgrades to a tarmac footpath running alongside an old millstream. Crossing the minor road at Holywell continue on the stream-side path to the road at the hamlet of Coombe. Go right up the hill past Frogend Farm, bearing left at The Hive and immediately right up the steep confined bridle-lane winding up to the Blackquarries Hill road. Maintain the ascent, passing the entrance to Warren Farm, enjoying delightful views into Tyley Bottom.

46

Entrance   to   the   Dawes   Almshouses

    As the lane eases its ascent, turn obliquely right along the farm lane, passing a padlocked post, installed to stop joyriding 4x4 vehicles. The lane curves with the scarp edge; existing waymarking guides walkers into the cattle pasture to contour just below the edge. The track descends into coniferous woodland and passing through an open space runs on down as a narrow footpath. As the bedrock switches to clay the path sinks into an amazingly deep holloway. At the bottom a stile gives entry into a fenced track. Go left to cross a road via opposing stiles.

    Cross the large field half-left, lower down glimpsing Alderley Trout Farm. At the far end a stile leads the path across the narrow corner of a pasture to a stile into Kennerwell Lane. Ascend the lane into Alderley; meeting a road, cross the ensuing crossways within the village. Notice the evergreen oak in the paddock on the right just before the next junction, and the parish church down to the right adjacent to Rose Hill Preparatory School. Go left, passing the grand, pale green- washed house to enter a short lane at a gate, to pursue the bridleway via stiles and gates, with the fence to the right, into the Kilcott valley.

47

MAP 20   KILCOTT MILL *to* HIGHFIELD LANE

Somerset   Monument

The Somerset Monument is a Beaufort family landmark. Erected in 1846, twenty years before the Tyndale Monument, it commemorates General Lord Somerset, a member of the Badminton family who served with commended zeal under Wellington at the Battle of Waterloo in 1815.

The bridleway descends in a lane to a gate to join Watery Lane, at the foot of Tresham combe. Go right to meet the valley road, turn left passing Kilcott Mill, accompanying the stream to just beyond the broad entrance to Lower Kilcott Farm, with its great mill ponds. Take the stile right at a gate; current waymarking directs the wayfarer farther along the road to ascend a bridleway through Claypit Wood.
      The path curves up the pasture, running upon a lynchet shelf shortly below a scrub bank, with superb views opening ahead into Long Combe. Proceeding via a stile, the path bears down half-left to the valley bottom by the hedge corner. Wending up the combe by a gateway, where a lynchet appears on the right, rise onto it, thereby reaching the head of the combe .
      The adoption of the Long Combe footpath is one of the major enhancements planned for the Cotswold Way. Here the walker may witness the wheeling buzzard, the running fox, hear the magpie, rook, pheasant and wood pigeon and really know the intimate beauty of the Cotswold edge in this, the quietest of re-entrant sanctuaries.

The long scarp-top village of Hawkesbury Upton has two pubs, The Fox and The Beaufort Arms, and a grocers store.

      A decrepit gate affording entry onto a muddy track rising within Frith Wood to a gate, soon the Somerset Monument appears ahead as the lane proceeds to link up with the original Cotswold Way and so meet the Hillesley road. Go left passing the impressive monument, now upon a footway advance to Hawkesbury Upton (shop and pubs), bear right short of the village at the village pond, passing Home Farm to bear left along Bath Lane, progressing onto the Highfield Lane road.

Long Combe

Stony Lane emerging from Long Combe

MAP 21   HIGHFIELD LANE to OLD SODBURY

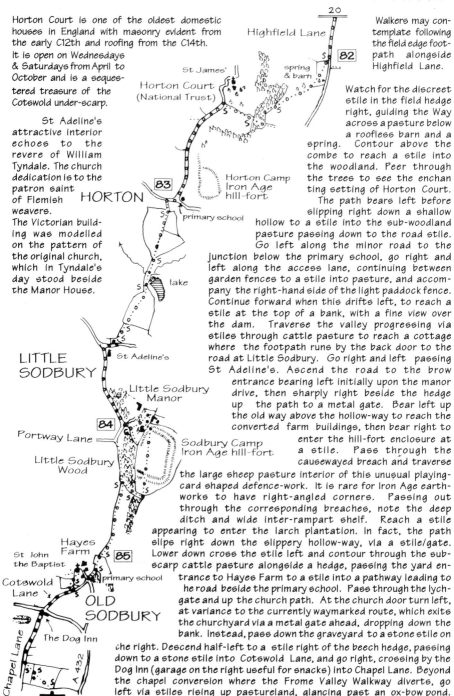

Horton Court is one of the oldest domestic houses in England with masonry evident from the early C12th and roofing from the C14th. It is open on Wednesdays & Saturdays from April to October and is a sequestered treasure of the Cotswold under-scarp.

St Adeline's attractive interior echoes to the revere of William Tyndale. The church dedication is to the patron saint of Flemish weavers. The Victorian building was modelled on the pattern of the original church, which in Tyndale's day stood beside the Manor House.

Walkers may contemplate following the field edge footpath alongside Highfield Lane.

Watch for the discreet stile in the field hedge right, guiding the Way across a pasture below a roofless barn and a spring. Contour above the combe to reach a stile into the woodland. Peer through the trees to see the enchanting setting of Horton Court. The path bears left before slipping right down a shallow hollow to a stile into the sub-woodland pasture passing down to the road stile. Go left along the minor road to the junction below the primary school, go right and left along the access lane, continuing between garden fences to a stile into pasture, and accompany the right-hand side of the light paddock fence. Continue forward when this drifts left, to reach a stile at the top of a bank, with a fine view over the dam. Traverse the valley progressing via stiles through cattle pasture to reach a cottage where the footpath runs by the back door to the road at Little Sodbury. Go right and left passing St Adeline's. Ascend the road to the brow entrance bearing left initially upon the manor drive, then sharply right beside the hedge up the path to a metal gate. Bear left up the old way above the hollow-way to reach the converted farm buildings, then bear right to enter the hill-fort enclosure at a stile. Pass through the causewayed breach and traverse the large sheep pasture interior of this unusual playing-card shaped defence-work. It is rare for Iron Age earthworks to have right-angled corners. Passing out through the corresponding breaches, note the deep ditch and wide inter-rampart shelf. Reach a stile appearing to enter the larch plantation. In fact, the path slips right down the slippery hollow-way, via a stile/gate. Lower down cross the stile left and contour through the sub-scarp cattle pasture alongside a hedge, passing the yard entrance to Hayes Farm to a stile into a pathway leading to he road beside the primary school. Pass through the lych-gate and up the church path. At the church door turn left, at variance to the currently waymarked route, which exits the churchyard via a metal gate ahead, dropping down the bank. Instead, pass down the graveyard to a stone stile on the right. Descend half-left to a stile right of the beech hedge, passing down to a stone stile into Cotswold Lane, and go right, crossing by the Dog Inn (garage on the right useful for snacks) into Chapel Lane. Beyond the chapel conversion where the Frome Valley Walkway diverts, go left via stiles rising up pastureland, glancing past an ox-bow pond.

St James' porch and the north wing of Horton Court

South entrance of Sodbury Camp

MAP 22   OLD SODBURY to HINTON HILL

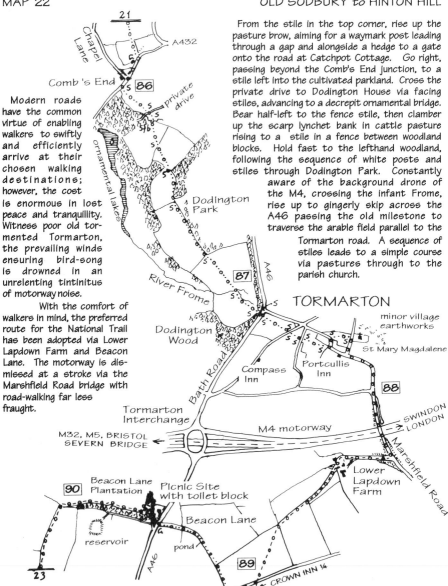

From the stile in the top corner, rise up the pasture brow, aiming for a waymark post leading through a gap and alongside a hedge to a gate onto the road at Catchpot Cottage. Go right, passing beyond the Comb's End junction, to a stile left into the cultivated parkland. Cross the private drive to Dodington House via facing stiles, advancing to a decrepit ornamental bridge. Bear half-left to the fence stile, then clamber up the scarp lynchet bank in cattle pasture rising to a stile in a fence between woodland blocks. Hold fast to the lefthand woodland, following the sequence of white posts and stiles through Dodington Park. Constantly aware of the background drone of the M4, crossing the infant Frome, rise up to gingerly skip across the A46 passing the old milestone to traverse the arable field parallel to the Tormarton road. A sequence of stiles leads to a simple course via pastures through to the parish church.

Modern roads have the common virtue of enabling walkers to swiftly and efficiently arrive at their chosen walking destinations; however, the cost is enormous in lost peace and tranquillity. Witness poor old tormented Tormarton, the prevailing winds ensuring bird-song is drowned in an unrelenting tintinitus of motorway noise.

With the comfort of walkers in mind, the preferred route for the National Trail has been adopted via Lower Lapdown Farm and Beacon Lane. The motorway is dismissed at a stroke via the Marshfield Road bridge with road-walking far less fraught.

Follow Marshfield Road out of the village, down the ramped road to Lower Lapdown Farm, with the handsome barn conversion to the left, passing through by a house on the right upon the bridle-track in a lane beside a long horse paddock, in the company of the Round Avon Ride. One field beyond the paddock end, bear half-left across the large field, aiming for the electricity pylon, to gain the country road. Go right and right again where a footpath crosses, with the hedge to the left (in the field just traversed). The path dips and enters a partially overgrown lane beside a pond rising to a the gate and a cautious crossing of the A46. Pass along the access road to the Picnic Site where there currently is a toilet block and frequently a refreshment caravan - re-alignment of the A46 threatens closure of this facility. Go left through the plantation and keep left beside the woodland to bear left as the path descends through a narrow gap, with the hedge to the right.

Once across the motorway bear left. Keep straight to the barn, curve left,

St Mary Magalene, Tormarton

Helen emerging from the Beacon Lane thicket

MAP 23   HINTON HILL to COLD ASHTON

set-aside pasture, and occasional motor-cross practice ground.

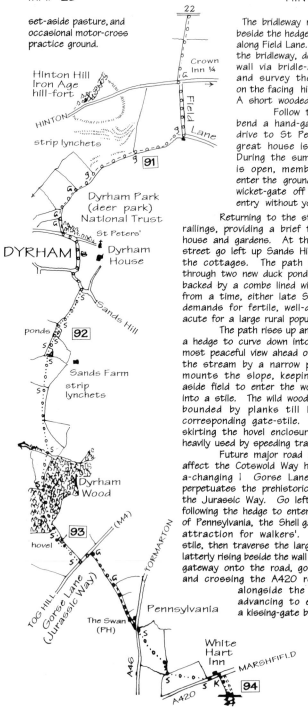

The bridleway runs along the crest of Hinton Hill beside the hedge to meet the road. Go left and right along Field Lane. Reaching the corner, bear right upon the bridleway, descending beside the tall Deer Park wall via bridle-and field-gates. Take your time and survey the extensive strip lynchet slopes on the facing hillside running down from the hill-fort. A short wooded hollow-way lane leads into Dyrham.

Follow the street left. At the right-hand bend a hand-gate gives access to the metalled drive to St Peters'. Normally locked when the great house is closed, its setting is exquisite. During the summer season, when Dyrham House is open, members of the National Trust may enter the grounds of this elegant house via the wicket-gate off the drive - don't even consider entry without your membership card !

Returning to the street, continue past the handsome railings, providing a brief tempting glimpse of the beautiful house and gardens. At the little triangle at the top of the street go left up Sands Hill, diverting right at a stile beyond the cottages. The path runs beside the hedge via stiles through two new duck pond enclosures below Sands Hill Farm, backed by a combe lined with yet more strip lynchets, dating from a time, either late Saxon or early Medieval, when the demands for fertile, well-drained ground for ploughing were acute for a large rural populace.

The path rises up an arable field to a stile, then beneath a hedge to curve down into the re-entrant valley, with a fine, most peaceful view ahead of Dyrham Wood. The path crosses the stream by a narrow plank rising to a hand-gate, then mounts the slope, keeping up left in the currently set-aside field to enter the woodland via a hand-gate converted into a stile. The wild woodland way ascends beside a stream bounded by planks till beyond a spring, leaving via a corresponding gate-stile. Advance with the field boundary skirting the hovel enclosure to reach Gorse Lane, currently heavily used by speeding traffic.

Future major road alignment of the A46 will radically affect the Cotswold Way here, so watch-out, trails they are a-changing ! Gorse Lane, like Bath and Campden Lanes, perpetuates the prehistoric Cotswold Ridgeway, often termed the Jurassic Way. Go left and then right through the gate following the hedge to enter a lane at a gate into the hamlet of Pennsylvania, the Shell garage and Swan Inn no doubt of some attraction for walkers'. Cross to the step-down stone stile, then traverse the large arable field on the long diagonal, latterly rising beside the wall to a stone stile. Bear half-left to a gateway onto the road, go left, passing the White Hart Inn, and crossing the A420 road proceed via the kissing-gate alongside the wall and beside a gravel drive, advancing to enter Holy Trinity churchyard at a kissing-gate beyond Whittington Farmhouse.

Dyrham means 'deer enclosure', perhaps of Roman origin. Pennsylvania suggests the establishment of an outlying or remote hamlet, while Cold Ashton describes 'the exposed place among ash trees'.

Dyrham House, gardens and Deer Park are wholly maintained by the National Trust. The elegant baroque style was the work of the French architect Samuel Hauduroy under the instructions of the owner, William Blathwayt, around the central Tudor hall that existed when, through marriage into the Winter family, he came to this handsome country retreat in 1686.

MAP 24

Pass through the churchyard via the corresponding kissing-gate, proceeding down the access lane to Cold Ashton's street. Go right, passing the Rectory and Manor, each grandly surveying the superb prospect down the St Catherine's valley, as indeed should any walker with a moments contemplative gaze. Continue with the road, leaving the village to cross the busy A46 directly into Greenway Lane (oddly signed as a plural). Future plans for the up-grading of this road will bring radical changes to the alignment of the Cotswold Way, which may accompany the first scenic paces of the Limestone Link Path down the St Catherine's valley before slipping into the Hamswell valley.

The metalled Greenway Lane advances into the secretive Hamswell dean. Note the strip lynchets that sneak into view over to the left before the road begins to wind purposefully downhill. Passing sadly neglected barns and Hill Farm bear right at the foot of the slope. Where the roadway swings left, fording St John's Brook and crossing successive stiles in a tiny spinney, hold to the lefthand hedgeline. Where this turns away left, continue straight across the pasture, with an angling lake down to the left, proceeding via intervening gates to reach a dutch-barn and muddy gate/stile onto a roadway at Lower Hamswell. Go left, passing a handsome vernacular house currently undergoing a thorough revitalisation. Bear right down the track, passing the anglers' parking area to a stile and track ford. Bear off right, immediately ascending the pasture bank rising to a stile, after which a welcome seat offers a fine excuse to rest and glance back over this quietly beautiful valley scene. Complete the ascent to a stile/padlocked hand-gate to enter the lane from Langridge. Go right within this delightful pitch-cobbled bridle-lane.

A gate spells the end of the confined lane, the track continuing beside the old wall. Where this ends, fork half-right up the rough way by a small wallstone quarry to the stone steps over the old field wall. With the wall on the right walk along the headland. The well documented Civil War battle of Lansdown of 5th July 1643 mentions this wall. The Parliamentary forces under Sir William Waller, defending Bath, bedraggled and depleted after an almost crushing defeat in the day's battle, crouched here before leaving fires to suggest an encampment, while they silently retreated to Bath in the gloaming. The path slips right, keeping just below the edge, and beside a moss-covered wall in light woodland, with a view down on Battlefields House. A stone-step stile switches the path on course to rise past the Grenvile Monument (English Heritage).

Continue along the green way through the pony paddock to a stile onto the Lansdown road. Cross straight over, bearing right with the metalled access roadway leading to the Avon Fire Service Headquarters. Skirt round following the high fence on a path which leads to a hand-gate. Contour the pasture below the wall, latterly fence, to the tip of the spur, clambering over the stile to stand beside the white-painted O.S. column on Hanging Hill (from hangra meaning 'the steep slope').

Follow the wall running south-eastwards, skirting an old quarry to reach a stile in the corner into a golf course enclosure, a northern extension of the Lansdown Golf Course. Keep by the fence, then wall, to cross a stile dropping onto the stone track. Go left uphill, keeping off the edge of the fairway.

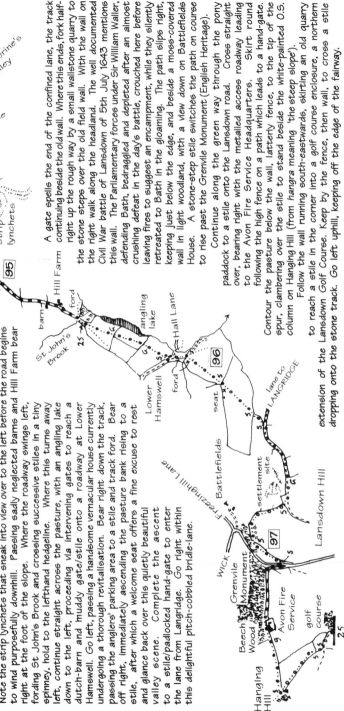

COLD ASHTON

Holy Trinity
Hyde's Lane
Manor House & Old Rectory
St Catherine's Valley
The Lynch
Slough Lane
A46
farm
strip lynchets
Greenway Lane
95
Hill Farm
barn
ford
St John's Brook
25
angling lake
Lower Hamswell
ford
Hall Lane
seat
96
lane to LANGRIDGE
Freezinghill Lane
Battlefields
settlement site
Lansdown Hill
WICK
Grenvile Monument
Beech Wood
Avon Fire Service
golf course
97
Hanging Hill
25

Cold Ashton Manor

St Catherine's valley from the Manor viewpoint

MAP 25
LANSDOWN HILL to WESTON

The track, lightly fenced off from the fairway, runs alongside the woodland of Further Slate. At a junction of tracks, go right passing barns, now with the golf course to the left and Pipley Wood on the right, and advance to a gate, the track slants downhill, the Cotswold Way branching left at the foot of the initial bank, rising gently to a stile/gate to contour below the lightly wooded scarp edge, which later doubled as the rampart of Little Down hill-fort. The path bears up left at a waymark post to join the greenway entering the hill-fort. At this point the Cotswold Way and Cotswold escarpment are geographically at their westernmost point. The view down over Pipley Bottom and the glasshouse of North Stoke features the winding river Avon running towards Keynsham and Bristol. Interestingly, the broad meadows at this point have Scandinavian names Holm and Mickle Mead, meaning respectively, 'raised' and 'big meadows'.

Enter the hill-fort at the gate, traversing the interior on an un-ploughed strip. Passing through the ramparts, bear right alongside the deep ditch, then swing left alongside the scarptop wall to a stile slipping behind the Bath Racecourse starting gates to reach Prospect Stile, with its topograph erected in 1990 by the Cotswold Warden Service. Climb the stile and bear left, briefly resting on the convenient bench before descending leftward to join a bridle-track running right beside a hedge down to the ridge-top crossing-point of a bridle-lane. Slip through the fenced passage, then go right, to a stile/ metal bridle-gate. Continuing along the ridge, confined by a fence, via a second bridle-gate/gap at the next path obstacle, bear up right on the duckboards to a stile as walkers and horse-riders are segregated, the path running in a hedge tunnel to a second stile near the path corner. At the corner a permissive path right leads up from a stile to the bedraggled clump surmounting Kelston Round Hill, a notable Avon valley viewpoint.

The bridle-lane and footpath are shortly segregated again, the footpath section terminating at a stile. Thereafter the often muddy way becomes far more agreeable underfoot as the limestone bedrock becomes more apparent on the descent of Dean Hill. The road joined, pass Deanhill Farm, branching right to a stile at the lefthand bend from where the road steeply descends. Cattle poached ground is traversed to a fence stile at the top of the pasture. Keeping beside the ridgetop fence, again the path is badly affected by loitering cattle before the path is relieved from the scrub-confined ridge, descending to the neglected O.S. column on Penn Hill. Continue the descent, watching for the path switch left by-passing a stile, to descend the pasture bank to a stile onto the recreation ground in Weston. Skirt to the right of the football pitch, traversing to the far corner where a kissing-gate puts the walker onto Penhill Road. Go left, descending to the pedestrian crossing of Weston High Street. Go right into Church Street, and follow the path rising into the churchyard. The beautiful interior of All Saints is worthy of a few minutes of any walker's time. Pass on through to Church Road ascending left, latterly via a confined path, to reach Purlewent Drive. Go right, bearing left in the cul-de-sac to follow the confined footpath running to the rear of the housing estate.

Eastern rampart of Little
Down Iron Age hill-fort

Companions consider the Warden's Topograph at Prospect Stile, Kelston Round Hill
dominates the view (old maps show a circular enclosure containing the summit trees).

MAP 26   WESTON to BATH ABBEY

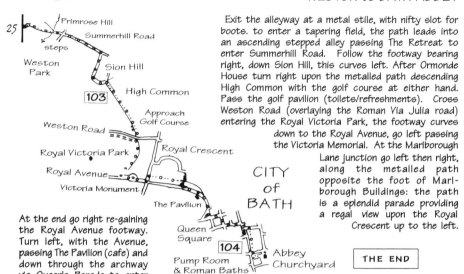

Exit the alleyway at a metal stile, with nifty slot for boots. to enter a tapering field, the path leads into an ascending stepped alley passing The Retreat to enter Summerhill Road. Follow the footway bearing right, down Sion Hill, this curves left. After Ormonde House turn right upon the metalled path descending High Common with the golf course at either hand. Pass the golf pavilion (toilets/refreshments). Cross Weston Road (overlaying the Roman Via Julia road) entering the Royal Victoria Park, the footway curves down to the Royal Avenue, go left passing the Victoria Memorial. At the Marlborough Lane junction go left then right, along the metalled path opposite the foot of Marlborough Buildings: the path is a splendid parade providing a regal view upon the Royal Crescent up to the left.

At the end go right re-gaining the Royal Avenue footway. Turn left, with the Avenue, passing The Pavilion (cafe) and down through the archway via Queen's Parade to enter Queen's Square. Go left in front of John Wood's grand house, keep right, pass the Lansdown Park & Ride bus stop. Bear left at the cycles-only entrance to Wood Street, pass through Quiet Street going right with New Bond Street, to enter the narrow pedestrian Bond Street Place continue over Upper Borough Walls into Union Passage, crossing Cheap Street via a corridor entering the Abbey Churchyard precinct. The finest journey's end of any long distance path in England.

THE END

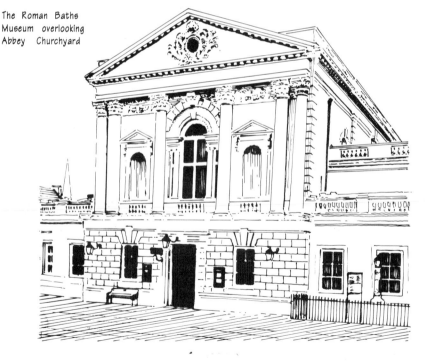

The Roman Baths Museum overlooking Abbey Churchyard

Bath Abbey soaring
over the Great Bath,
viewpoint within the
Roman Baths Museum.

PLACE-NAME INDEX - page number in bold followed by the map number

YOUR PERSONAL RECORD OF THE WALK

DATE	ENCOUNTERS, CONDITIONS & COMPANIONS . . .

REARDON PUBLISHING

56 Upper Norwood St, Leckhampton, CHELTENHAM, Gloucestershire
GL53 ODU

Reardon Publishing is a family run Publishing House based in Cheltenham, producing guides to the Cotswold area using both local authors
and printers. So when you buy a Reardon guidebook it really is a local
guide, and by purchasing these guides you are supporting the local
economy.

"The Cotswold Way" is just one in the series of "Walkabout" guides
covering some of the best walking in the Cotswolds. If you have enjoyed
it and would like to know what other titles are available, then please
send a large stamped (2 x First Class) addressed envelope to the
above address for our free illustrated booklist and mail order details.

Also available mail order is the beautifully hand-drawn and fully
illustrated map of the Cotswold Way created by the author MARK
RICHARDS (see opposite page). This souvenir map of the walk is
perfectly suited for framing and can act as a keepsake of your
walk through some of the best countryside England has to offer.
Just send a cheque for £9.95 made payable to "REARDON
PUBLISHING" and within days your map will be safely on its way to you.

KEEP THE COUNTRY CODE
